PRACTICAL JOKES

What's your talent?

I can easy learn all the lyrics to all my favorite songs, but I can retain a single thing from my math class…

Two blondes, one to other:

- I met a cute guy and we're together for over a year. He is sweet and kind to me, but he doesn't propose…I don't know what to do.
- Honey, I think he is smart too.

It's too bad that most of the people use their head to wash them off.

The ideal man doesn't drink, smoke, cheat, swear and he doesn't exist.

In a church two people celebrate a wedding. The priest comes closer to the man and he says:

- Do you shed of Satan?
- No, answers the man.
- Why? Are you sure?
- Well, someone has to cook for me, right?

My wife's cat died, so I got her a similar one. She got mad and yelled at me: "What the hell am I supposed to do with two dead cats?"

A man decided to become a complete new person, so he gave his seat on the bus to a blind old lady.

He lost his job as a bus driver.

This morning I ran out of paper so I used the newspaper. All I can say is that the times are rough…

A horse walks in a restaurant. The waiter comes at the table: "Hey, sir!"

"No, no. Just a coffee, I just ate."

The husband told his wife about his exes. She asks:

"Honey, at least I'm glad I was your first ginger girlfriend!"

"Dear, why do you think I'm going to hell? All of them were gingers…"

If you want to mess with a bartender's head order a virgin Long Island Ice Tea.

For most of the people, prison is one word, but for others is a complete sentence.

Let's celebrate the National Weed Appreciation Day, or how my friends like to call it " My whole week".

- Honey, go to the shop and take some vegetables for the soup.
- Are you nuts? It's 0 degree outside. I'm freezing and neither with the dog can't I go outside.
- Did I tell you to take the dog with you?

Today I cooked. I start to slice some onion and I looked in my wallet too. I didn't want to cry twice.

A gypsy with her husband is in bed. She tells him:

- **Give me your hand. I want to read before I sleep.**

Today my psychiatrist gave me a diagnostic. I'm a homophobic homosexual. He suggests me to not beat myself up about it.

The bride was so nervous about the wedding that she started make rehearsal with her neighbor.

Schrodinger takes his cat to the vet for the monthly check up.

The doctor comes to him and says:

- **I have some bad news for you.**
- **What happened…**
- **Sir, you don't have a cat.**

What the cannibal eats before going to the therapist?

A piece of mind.

How do you make something out of nothing?

Ask your wife!

What's the difference between a painter and a pizza?

The pizza can feed a family of four.

What's the difference between a sad person and a happy person?

The sad person is married and has 3 kids

I met a couple that stick to each other from the beginning. They met at the glue factory.

They are inseparable since then.

What's difference between kitties and orphans?

The kittens actually get adopted.

A woman to another:

- Dear do you talk to your husband when you make love?

- Yes, if he calls me.

Brother, do you think in heaven women and men are separated?

- Well why do you think it's called heaven?

What's the difference between guilt and shame?

- **You are guilty when you sleep with your friend's wife, but it's a shame to not too.**

How old you were when you enter first time on your parents?

- 20…

Dear, did you put a password to our fridge? Why?

- Do you think I don't know how you sneak at the midnight to eat cookies?
- Oh, god. What's the password?
- Our wedding date.
- Shit…

On a dating app a man put in his description: "I want a wife".

He got a lot of similar answers: "Take mine!"

How make a woman to go nuts? Give her your card in the time of pandemic, when the mall is closed.

Finally, it's Friday. Tonight I'm going out.

To throw the trash and back.

Honey, the colleagues from work told me I'm fat.

- **Baby, don't mind them. Now get those 2 chairs and come next to me.**

- My friend, my mother in law is like a treasure.
- What do you mean?
- You have this constant feeling that you need to bury her.

The political system makes you work your ass off until your 65 years. Be free. Die before.

The marriage is the only war where enemies sleep together.

If the stress burned calories, God, I'd be a model by now.

I like my men how I like my coffee: hot, cheap and Irish.

I finally got my heart's crush. I still don't know what to do with the rest of the body.

I met the parents of my boyfriend yesterday. We find out we're both adopted and brothers…

Everyone's says that without losing, you can't learn anything. My sister got cancer and lost. She didn't learn anything.

What's the favorite bar of the tyhpographers?

The space bar.

Today I bought myself a First Aid Kit. I thought I'd treat myself a bit.

I was fighting with my husband and he told me:

- I know you think I don't respect your privacy…
- How do you know that?
- Well, that's what you wrote in your dairy.

    My dad told me this:
- This is the happiest day of your life. Don't ever forget this day.

    It was the day before my wedding.

I went to the doctors recently.
He said: "Don't eat anything fatty"
I said: "What, like bacon and burgers?"
He said, "No, fatty. Don't eat anything!"

Five guys sit a table in a bar. One says:

- I really wonder if someone from our group is gay.

One of them answers:

- **I really wonder too, 'because Daniel is too cute.**

Did you hear about the farmer that won an award?

He was exceptional in his field!

Dark humor is like a child with cancer…it's never get old.

Losing my virginity was like a hockey game. It hurt a lot, but at least all my family showed up.

Last week I went at therapist. He recommended me to not show up anymore, because he is nuts too now.

A husband to his wife:

- **Honey do you know how lucky you are?**
- **Why, honey?**
- **Because you have me.**

When I wished a life like a TV show, I didn't expect it to be a comedy one.

Better days are coming. They are called Saturday and Sunday.

The husband almost dying…"My love, I have to confess something. I cheated you with your best friend."

- I know love, that's why I poisoned you.

Women are incredible beings. They are succeed to forgive you, even if you did nothing wrong.

Your depression comes to the fact that you don't smoke, you don't drink and you see the world exactly how it is.

Everyone should believe in something. I believe I can drink one more.

My mom called me yesterday.
- What do you do?
- I burn calories.
- Oh, are you working out?
- No, I fry some meat.

The coffee is something exceptional, you know? Many children came in this world due to expression: "Do you want to go out for a coffee?"

I'd wish 2 holidays of 6 months per year.

A woman walks into a library and asked if they had any books about paranoia.

Librarian: "They're right behind you!!".

My mom is on seafood diet. She sees food and eats it.

David used to be addicted to soap, but now it's clean.

Why koalas aren't actual bears?

They don't meet the qualifications.

What do you call a boomerang that doesn't come back?

A stick.

My wife and I were happy twenty five years. Then we met.

Two blondes are talking:

- I can't wait to go in Venice.
- Why? You were 3 years ago.
- Yeah, but the streets were flooded.

A man walks in a bar and ask the waiter: "Do you receive orders?"
He answers: "Yes, sir."
The man says: "Down!"

I quit smoking today.

If I will have money, I will start again.

My boyfriend gave me a cryogenic rose and he says he will come back after the petals of the rose will fall off.

A new scandal in hospital appears on newspaper. The cockroaches took head lice from bed bugs.

In a hospital, the doctor asks the man diagnosed with cranial fracture:
- **Married?**
- **No, just an accident.**

My child had learned 25 letters from the alphabet, but she can retain one. I don't know Y.

What should you do if you're cold? Stand in the corner. It's 90 degrees.

A guy enters in a bar and he approach a girl:

"Hey, girl. Do you want my sweater? It's boyfriend material."

When Aphrodite stands naked on a giant clam, she's "beautiful" and a "goddess", but when I do it, I'm "drunk" and "no longer allowed in the aquarium."

- Have you heard the news?
- No, what happened?
- The CEO of Pepsi got caught with too much coke.

I lost my parents last year. What a great poker game it was.

What Sully and a carrot have in common?

One is funny beast and the other is a bunny feast.

Joe is calling her girlfriend, Jennifer:

- Jen, can you come at my house?
- No, I can't. I'm hiding a body.
- Well, my parents are not home so..
- I know.

At my boss's funeral, kneeling and whispering at coffin:
"Who's thinking outside the box now Mike?"

I wanted to tell you a gay joke, but I wouldn't tell you straight in the face.

Why is the sky blue?

No one bother to ask him how is feeling…

I asked my mom today:

- Mom, why did you marry my father?
- I can't believe even my child asks this.

I told my father I finally passed a test, but he looked at me disappointed after I told him it was the pregnancy test.

Printed in Great Britain
by Amazon